The
Winning Life

An Introduction to Buddhist Practice

World Tribune
Press

© 2016 SGI-USA

Published by World Tribune Press
606 Wilshire Blvd.
Santa Monica, CA 90401

Cover and interior design © Lightbourne, Inc.

ISBN: 978-1-944604-03-5

Printed in the United States of America

22   21   20   19   18   2   3   4   5   6   7

Illustration credits:
Getty Images/Trina Dalziel, pp. iv, 6, 16, 18, 20, 23, 25, 27, 46, 47, 48,
123RF/Rudall, p. 8, Shutterstock/Bioraven, p. 9, 123RF/Sonya Illustration, p. 15,
123RF/Betelgejze, p. 11, Shutterstock/Tatsiana Tsyhanova, p. 32,
Shutterstock/Makar, p. 51, Shutterstock/Plearn, p. 55,
123RF/Elena Pimonova, p. 57, Shutterstock/Kamenuka, p. 59

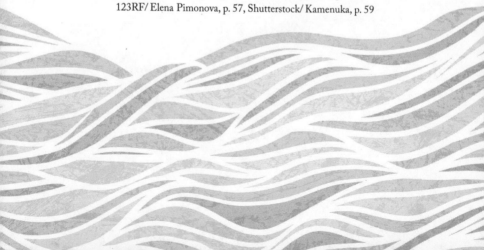

Contents

each
of us
possesses the
potential for a
winning life

The Winning Life

E ACH OF US POSSESSES THE POTENTIAL FOR A winning life. Within us is the ability to live with courage, to have fulfilling relationships, to enjoy good health and prosperity, to feel and show true compassion for others, and to face and surmount our deepest problems.

Crucial to living a winning life is to undergo an inner transformation that will enable us to bring out our noblest human virtues and thereby change our circumstances. This process is a revolution of our own character, an individual human revolution.

Consider the following scenario: Perhaps you feel underappreciated at work. Maybe your boss is belligerent or ignores you. After a while you develop a chip on your shoulder. Though you may be an expert at hiding negativity, every once in a while it rears its ugly head.

Perhaps your co-workers or boss perceive you in turn as not being entirely committed to the success of your job, or that you have a bad attitude. Of course there are myriad reasons for your "bad" attitude and all of them valid. But whatever the reasons, you miss opportunities for advancement, maybe even lose your job, because of the poor relationship. This is a common scenario in today's working environment.

But suppose you start coming to work with a new attitude that is not just a mental adjustment but an outlook bolstered by a deep sense of vitality, confidence, and compassion, and based upon serious self-reflection. Your compassion leads you to have empathy for your boss's situation. Armed with a new understanding, you treat your boss differently, offering support and finding yourself less and less discouraged by any negativity he or she may display toward you.

Your boss begins to see you in a new light. Opportunities present themselves.

This is obviously a very simple example and many of us would say this is a natural thing to do, but to live this way every day requires the ability to make and sustain basic changes in our hearts and character. Once the change is made, like a never-ending domino effect, we can have continual positive impact on the people around us.

A CHANGE ON THE INSIDE
CHANGES OUR ENVIRONMENT

The practice of Buddhism as taught by Nichiren Daishonin is a catalyst for experiencing this inner revolution. It provides us with immediate access to the unlimited potential inherent in our lives by which we can live a winning life.

It is the promise of Nichiren Buddhism that we can attain a state of freedom and unshakable happiness for ourselves while creating harmony with others.

Buddhism is a way of life that—on the most fundamental level—makes no distinction between the individual human being and the environment in which that person lives. Like a fish in water, the two are not only inseparable, but each serves as a catalyst for the other. Thus, to a Buddhist, self-improvement and enhancement of our circumstances go hand in hand. The two are actually so interlocked that it is incorrect to consider them separate entities. In treating the sufferings and delusions of human beings, there is the accompanying benefit of better social conditions, since the one is the source of the other—for better or worse.

While the word *Buddha* may conjure up images of a specific person from history or world religions courses we have taken, it is also a description

We can attain a state of freedom and unshakable happiness for ourselves while creating harmony with others.

of the highest state of life each of us can experience. *Buddha* actually means "awakened one," and the historical Buddha (known as Shakyamuni or Siddhartha Gautama) discovered that all humans have a potential for enlightenment—or Buddhahood—in the depths of their lives. This could be likened to a rosebush in winter: the flowers are dormant even though we know that the bush contains the potential to bloom.

Similarly, by tapping into our potential, we can find unlimited wisdom, courage, hope, confidence, compassion, vitality, and endurance. Instead of avoiding or fearing our problems, we learn to confront them with joyful vigor, confident in our ability to surmount whatever life throws in our path.

Buddhism also shows us the most satisfying way to live among others. It explains that when we help others overcome their problems, our own lives are expanded. When our capacity increases and our character is strengthened, the source of our problems comes under our control. Because we make an internal change, our relationship with our problems changes as well, wresting positive resolutions in any number of astounding yet tangible ways.

CULTIVATE YOUR INNER POWER THROUGH BUDDHIST PRACTICE

Through this process of inner reformation, we can also fulfill our dreams and desires. Rather than calling for the eradication of desires, Nichiren Buddhism recognizes that to be human means to have desires and that as we proceed in our human revolution we elevate our state of life, "magnetizing" our lives to attract that which will further our happiness.

Not only do we fulfill our desires as we change ourselves through Buddhist practice, but the very pursuit of those desires through our practice is like rocket fuel propelling us toward our enlightenment.

Life is ever-changing, moment to moment. The only constant in life is change. Our minds are constantly in flux, and while one minute we may have the courage to conquer the world, the next minute we can be overwhelmed by even the simplest occurrences. But through our steady, daily practice, we continually strengthen our resolve and ability to live a winning life.

Buddhism unleashes our inherent power to take on all of life's challenges and win.

Winning in life, however, is not the absence or avoidance of problems. Being human, almost by definition, means we will constantly meet up with challenges. True happiness or victory in life is having the tools to take on each hurdle, overcome it, and become stronger and wiser in the process. Inside each human being is a storehouse of all the necessary traits to tackle every problem that confronts us. Buddhism is the practice that allows us access to this storehouse and unleashes our inherent power to take on all of life's challenges and win.

The Practice

THERE ARE THREE BASICS IN APPLYING Buddhism: faith, practice, and study. They are the primary ingredients in the recipe for developing our innate enlightened condition, or Buddhahood. All three are essential. With this recipe, we will experience actual proof of our transformation in the forms of both conspicuous and inconspicuous benefit. The recipe is universal.

1. FAITH

Faith in Nichiren Buddhism is grounded in one's personal experience of applying Buddhism and seeing improvements in the quality of one's life, what we call benefit.

Nichiren Buddhism thus emphasizes obtaining "actual proof" of the teaching's power. Faith begins as an expectation or hope that something will happen when we start to practice;

it's an open-mindedness to the vast potential within us and to the power of Buddhist practice to help us fulfill that potential. At the start of our journey, if we are willing to try the practice and anticipate some result, we will then develop our faith brick by brick as examples of actual proof accrue.

2. PRACTICE

To develop faith, we must take action. We strengthen our wisdom and vital life force by actualizing our Buddhahood each day in a very concrete way. Practice in Nichiren Buddhism consists of two parts: practice for ourselves and practice for others.

Practice for ourselves is primarily the chanting of Nam-myoho-renge-kyo. Each morning and evening, along with chanting Nam-myoho-renge-kyo, we recite from two significant chapters of the Lotus Sutra—chapters which explain that each individual holds the potential for enlightenment and that life itself is eternal. This daily practice is referred to as *gongyo* (literally "assiduous practice"). (How-to-chant videos are available in the member resources section of our website, www.sgi-usa.org.)

Practice for others consists of personal efforts based on

compassion to enable others to believe in the great, unrealized potential of their lives. Practice for others takes many forms, but the most basic is to share Nichiren Buddhism with them. Called *shakubuku*, this is an act of the utmost respect and concern for others. The development of our compassion through such practice for others is also a direct benefit to us.

3. STUDY

To gain confidence that this practice is valid and to understand why your efforts will bring about a result, it is essential to study the tenets of this Buddhism. The basis of study comes from the founder himself, Nichiren Daishonin. More than 700 years ago, he instructed followers in the correct way to practice; and his writings, which have been preserved and translated into English, give us valuable insight into how this practice will benefit us today.

The Soka Gakkai International, a worldwide association that supports practitioners of Nichiren Buddhism, has prepared numerous study materials that offer deeper looks at Buddhist theory, as well as practical applications through members' testimonies. There are also English translations of the original teachings of Buddhism, such as the Lotus Sutra. By helping to build understanding and confidence, the study material provides vital encouragement for us—especially at crucial moments. (www.nichirenlibrary.org provides access to the Lotus Sutra and Nichiren's letters.)

In the United States, the primary study material is the *World Tribune* newspaper and its monthly supplement, *Living Buddhism*. Regular brief readings, even twenty minutes a day, provide a strong foundation for one's faith and practice. (Visit www.worldtribune.org for more information.)

WHAT IS NAM-MYOHO-RENGE-KYO?

The basic prayer or chant is Nam-myoho-renge-kyo. This is the name of the Mystic Law that permeates life eternally throughout the universe. Nichiren Daishonin revealed this Law as the underlying principle contained in Buddhism's highest teaching, the Lotus Sutra. All life is an expression or manifestation of this

Nam-myoho-renge-kyo is the name of the Mystic Law.

Law. Thus when we chant this Mystic Law, we attune our lives to the perfect rhythm of the universe. The result is increased vital life force, wisdom, compassion, and good fortune to face the challenges in front of us.

The translation of Nam-myoho-renge-kyo is as follows:

NAM—Devotion. By devoting our lives to this Law through our faith, practice, and study, we will awaken the life condition of Buddha, or enlightenment, inside ourselves.

MYOHO—Mystic Law. As Nichiren explained in one of his writings: "What then does *myo* signify? It is simply the mysterious nature of our life from moment to moment, which the mind cannot comprehend or words express. When we look into our own mind at any moment, we perceive neither color nor form to verify that it exists. Yet we still cannot say it does not exist, for many differing thoughts continually occur. The mind cannot be considered either to exist or not to exist. Life is indeed an elusive reality that transcends both the words and concepts of existence and nonexistence. It is neither existence nor nonexistence, yet exhibits the qualities of both. It is the mystic entity of the Middle Way that is the ultimate reality. *Myo* is the name given to the mystic nature of life, and *ho*, to its manifestations" (*The Writings of Nichiren Daishonin*, vol. 1, p. 4).

RENGE—Literally, the lotus flower, which produces both flower and fruit at the same time. This represents the simultaneity of cause and effect. We create causes through thoughts, words, and actions. With each cause made, an effect is registered simultaneously in the depths of life, and those effects are manifested when we meet the right environmental circumstances. Life itself is an endless series of causes and simultaneous effects. Chanting Nam-myoho-renge-kyo is the deepest cause we can make in order to produce our desired effect.

KYO—Sound or teaching. This is how the Buddha has traditionally instructed—through the spoken word, which is heard.

Myoho-renge-kyo is the Lotus Sutra's title and contains its essential meaning. Nichiren Daishonin added *namu* (contracted to *nam*), which comes from Sanskrit. Thus by chanting Nam-myoho-renge-kyo, we express our devotion to the Lotus Sutra's essential teaching that all people are endowed with the wonderful virtues of a Buddha: unlimited compassion, wisdom, courage, and happiness. Nam-myoho-renge-kyo is the ultimate invocation of life that brings forth this potential.

WHAT DO WE CHANT FOR?

There are no prerequisites or rules as to what to chant for. We simply make the decision to begin chanting Nam-myoho-renge-kyo. And by chanting, we begin to experience the energy and wisdom to find a deep and abiding peace and happiness within.

In the sixty years since this Buddhism has been widely accessible through the efforts of the Soka Gakkai worldwide, millions have chanted about every conceivable problem and goal, from the most dire health and financial crises to the most urgent matters of the heart. We also regularly chant for the happiness of our family and friends.

When we chant, we are not praying to an external deity invested with human qualities like judgment. Our prayers are communicated into the depths of our being when we invoke the sound of the Mystic Law.

This universal Law is impartial, and no prayer is more or less worthy than another. The only issue is whether we can create value in our lives and help others to do the same. As Nichiren teaches, we experience enlightenment through a continual transformation that takes place in the depths of our existence as we seek to fulfill our desires, bring out our noblest virtues, and resolve our conflicts.

It is important to understand that our prayers are realized because we bring forth from within ourselves the highest life condition and the wisdom to take correct action. In that sense, prayers embody a determination such as "I will accomplish this" rather than wishing for something to happen. Such a determined attitude acknowledges that we already inherently possess everything we need to accomplish our goals or construct a happy life.

A MIRROR FOR ONE'S LIFE

To begin one's practice and experience its full benefit, one applies to receive the Gohonzon, the object of devotion for Nichiren Buddhism.

Nichiren Daishonin inscribed his enlightenment in the form of a mandala called the Gohonzon, and believers chant Nam-myoho-renge-kyo to a scroll form of the Gohonzon enshrined in their own homes. (For information on how to receive the Gohonzon, please ask your sponsor or contact the SGI organization at 310-260-8900 or www.sgi-usa.org.)

In the Gohonzon, Nichiren graphically depicted his enlightenment, or Buddhahood, which is the enlightened state of the universe. The important point here is that the same potential for enlightenment exists within each of us. And as we chant to the Gohonzon, we tap into that enlightened life condition, our own Buddhahood. This is why Nichiren calls the Gohonzon a mirror for the inner self. It is a way to see inside, to begin changing what we don't like and strengthening what we do like. We have the potential of many life conditions, which appear when we come in contact with various external stimuli. For instance, the presence or thought of a loved one stimulates positive emotions. To bring out our highest potential condition of life, our Buddhahood, we also need a

When we chant Nam-myoho-renge-kyo to the Gohonzon, we tap into our own Buddhahood.

stimulus. As our conviction develops, we
will come to see that the Gohonzon is
the most positive external stimulus, and
chanting Nam-myoho-renge-kyo to it is
the internal cause that will activate the
latent state of Buddhahood in our lives.

The scroll of the Gohonzon is kept in
an altar in the practitioner's home where
it can be protected from the daily routine
of the household.

HOW OFTEN DO WE CHANT?

Our basic practice, which includes chanting Nam-myoho-
renge-kyo, reciting sections of the Lotus Sutra, and
offering silent prayers, is carried out each morning and evening.
Chanting Nam-myoho-renge-kyo, the primary practice, is
like fuel for an engine. Reciting the sutra is a supplementary
practice, like adding oil to that engine. When the two are
combined, it is most effective, and we feel the confidence of
performing in top condition.

We are also free to chant as often as we like and to our
heart's content. Most new practitioners will experiment with
chanting until they experience something tangible, sort of like
a test drive. The duration of any particular chanting session
is up to each individual's preferences from as little as five to
ten minutes to one hour or more. The more we put into it, the

more we will get out of it. The complete morning and evening practice, however, should become the basis of our daily practice, a special time when we can reaffirm our determinations and harmonize directly with the rhythm of the universe.

HELPING AND PRAYING FOR OTHERS

As we start to see actual proof of the power of our Buddhist practice, we naturally come to share our experiences with friends and encourage them to try chanting Nam-myoho-renge-kyo as well. In fact, this sharing with others, or *shakubuku*, is a key to receiving benefit and developing our inner potential for enlightenment, or Buddhahood.

The SGI's ultimate purpose is to contribute to the establishment of a peaceful world.

The SGI's ultimate purpose is to contribute to the establishment of a peaceful world where all people experience happiness. We can experience a more expansive and stronger life condition by endeavoring to help others. This way of life founded on compassion is instrumental in helping us strengthen our own Buddha nature. It is the altruistic interaction with people in our daily lives that will help us grow and become enlightened.

This is not only Buddhist theory—most people recognize the satisfaction and growth that accompany their efforts to truly help others. Practicing Buddhism to overcome our own problems or circumstances gives us insight we can share. We can chant for our families and friends, we can encourage others to practice, we can begin to show our own transformation so that others will be encouraged to find out the source of our great changes and newfound personal freedom.

The Process

THE BUDDHA NATURE IS NOT JUST A HAPPY feeling or existential bliss; it is an actual state of life based on the Mystic Law of the universe. We do not need to understand exactly how this Mystic Law works before we can make use of it to our advantage. Laws of nature require neither our understanding nor our belief in them. Although we cannot see the law of gravity, we can attest to its existence. The Law of life (Mystic Law), which Buddhism postulates, is far too profound to be fully discussed here. Nonetheless, a few basic concepts can be explained as follows:

OUR LIVES ARE ETERNAL

Some religions teach that we live only one lifetime, and when we die, we go permanently to some beautiful hereafter such as heaven or some horrific eternal torture chamber known as hell. Some people believe there is nothing after death; this life is all there is. Buddhism's view of eternal life, however, posits that one's

We live many lifetimes, repeating the cycle of birth and death.

life or essence has no real beginning or end. We live many lifetimes, repeating the cycle of birth and death. Like going to sleep at night, we refresh our lives (death) and wake up anew (birth). This idea of life's energy neither being created nor destroyed but simply changing form is remarkably consistent with science.

Buddhism explains that our lives possess an eternal and unchanging aspect. When we die, our life

Death becomes the potential for life.

functions may stop, but the essence of our lives—our eternal identity, with myriad causes engraved in it—continues in a form that cannot be seen. Death then becomes the potential for life. Again, death is just like a rosebush in winter, dormant but containing the potential for flowers (life) within. And when the correct external circumstances are present, the roses will bloom (birth).

Everything we've done until this moment adds up to who we are. This is the law of cause and effect. For every cause, there must be an effect. This is karma. We make myriad causes every day through our thoughts, words, and actions, and for each cause, we receive an effect.

Buddhism says that, in essence, this law of cause and effect is simultaneous. The moment a cause is created, an effect is registered like a seed planted in the depths of life. In fact, this law is symbolized by the lotus flower, which flowers and fruits at the same time. While the effect is planted the same instant the cause is created, it may not appear instantly. When the correct external circumstances appear, the effect will then transform from potential to actual. Looked at another way, our karma is like a bank account of latent positive and negative effects we'll experience when our lives meet the right environmental conditions.

As we live our lives (making causes), effects accumulate within us, and when we die, those effects dictate the circumstances of our birth in the next life. When we are reborn, therefore, we will still face the same problems or karma from causes we have made. This goes a long way to explaining why people are born under such different circumstances—in other words, why people have different karma.

This principle suggests we can change our karma or destiny that we may have thought unchangeable. Since we've made the causes to be in our present circumstances, we can make the causes necessary to improve them. This is the great hope and promise offered by Buddhist practice. While in theory all we have to do is make the best causes to get the best effects, many times we feel we have little control over the causes we make. A prime example is when we get angry at and say something we don't really mean to people who are close to us. At such times, the condition of anger may seem more powerful than our general nature. When we practice Buddhism, however, we can establish Buddhahood as our basic condition of life and face our circumstances filled with wisdom and compassion. We can master our anger rather than be mastered by it. The concept of the Ten Worlds offers insights into how this is so.

> *When we practice Buddhism, we can establish Buddhahood as our basic condition of life and face our circumstances filled with wisdom and compassion.*

OUR LIVES HAVE TEN WORLDS

One way that Buddhism explains life is through a concept known as the Ten Worlds. These are ten states or conditions of life that we experience within ourselves and which are then reflected in all aspects of our lives. Each of us possesses the potential for all ten, and we shift from one to another at any moment. That is, at each moment, one of the Ten Worlds is being manifested and the other nine are dormant. From lowest to highest, they are:

Hell—This is a state of suffering and despair, in which we perceive we are powerless, having no freedom of action. It is characterized by the impulse to destroy ourselves and everything around us.

Hunger—Hunger is the state of being controlled by insatiable desire for money, power, status, or whatever. While desires are inherent in any of the Ten Worlds, in this state we are at the mercy of our cravings and cannot control them or ever satisfy them.

Animality—In this state, we are ruled by instinct. We exhibit neither reason nor moral sense nor the ability to make long-range judgments. In the world of animality, we operate by the law of the jungle, so to speak. We will not hesitate to take advantage of those weaker than ourselves and fawn on those who are stronger.

Anger—In this state, awareness of ego emerges, but it is a selfish, greedy, distorted ego, determined to best others at all costs and seeing everything as a potential threat to itself. In this state, we value only ourselves and tend to hold others in contempt. We are strongly attached to the idea of our own superiority and cannot bear to admit that anyone exceeds us in anything.

Humanity—This is a flat, passive state of life, from which we can easily shift into the lower four worlds. While we may generally behave in a humane fashion in this state, we are highly vulnerable to external influences.

Heaven—This is a state of intense joy stemming, for example, from the fulfillment of some desire, a sense of physical well-being, or inner contentment. Though intense, the joy experienced in this state is short-lived and dependent on external influences.

The six states from hell to heaven have in common the fact that their emergence or disappearance is governed by external circumstances. Any happiness or satisfaction to be gained in these states depends totally upon circumstances and is therefore transient and subject to change. The next two states, voice-hearers and cause-awakened ones, come about when we recognize that everything experienced in the six lower worlds is impermanent, and we begin to seek some lasting truth and a more resilient happiness. These two states, plus the next two— bodhisattva and Buddhahood—are not passive reactions to the environment like the first six. These higher states require deliberate effort to experience.

Voice-hearers (also called learning)—In this state, we seek the truth through the teachings or experience of others.

Cause-awakened ones (or realization)—This state is similar to voice-hearers, except that we seek the truth not through others' teachings but through our own direct perception of the world.

Having realized the impermanence of things, people in these two states have won a measure of independence and are no longer prisoner to their own reactions as in the lower worlds. However, they often tend to be contemptuous of people who have not yet reached this understanding. In addition, their search for truth is primarily self-oriented, so there is a great potential for egotism in these two states; and they may become satisfied with their progress without discovering the highest potential of human life in the ninth and tenth worlds.

Bodhisattva—Bodhisattvas are those who aspire to experience enlightenment and at the same time are equally determined to enable all other beings to do the same. Conscious of the bonds that link us to all others, in this state we realize that any happiness we alone enjoy is incomplete, and we devote ourselves to alleviating others' suffering. Those in this state find their greatest satisfaction in altruistic behavior.

Bodhisattvas realize that any happiness enjoyed alone is incomplete.

The states from hell to bodhisattva are collectively termed the nine worlds. This expression is often used in contrast to the tenth world, the enlightened state of Buddhahood.

Buddhahood—Buddhahood is a dynamic state that is difficult to describe. We can partially describe it as a state of completeness and perfect freedom, in which one is able to savor a sense of unity with the life force of the cosmos. Infinite compassion, boundless wisdom, and unwavering courage also characterize this state. For a person in the state of Buddhahood, everything—including the inevitable trials of aging, sickness, and death—can be experienced as an opportunity for joy and fulfillment. The inner life state of Buddhahood makes itself visible through altruistic commitment and actions enacted in the world of bodhisattva.

OUR LIVES CAN MANIFEST BUDDHAHOOD

The Ten Worlds were originally thought of as distinct physical realms into which beings were born as a result of accumulated karma. For example, human beings were born in the world of humanity, animals in the world of animality, and gods in the world of heaven. In Nichiren Buddhism, the Ten Worlds are instead viewed as conditions of life that all people have the potential to experience. At any moment, one of the ten will be manifest and the other nine dormant, but there is always the potential for change.

This principle is further expressed as the mutual possession of the Ten Worlds—the concept that each of the Ten Worlds possesses all ten within itself. For example, a person now in the state of hell may, at the next moment, either remain in hell or manifest any of the other nine states. The vital implication of this principle is that all people, in whatever state of life, have the ever-present potential to manifest Buddhahood. And equally important is that Buddhahood is found within the reality of our lives in the other nine worlds, not somewhere separate.

In the course of a day, we experience different states from moment to moment in response to our interaction with the environment. The sight of another's suffering may call forth the compassionate world of bodhisattva, and the loss of a loved one will plunge us into hell. However, all of us have one or more worlds around which our life activities usually center and to which we tend to revert when external stimuli subside. This is one's basic life tendency, and it has been established by each individual through prior actions. The purpose of Buddhist practice is to elevate one's basic life tendency and eventually establish Buddhahood as one's fundamental state.

Through Buddhist practice, the effects of karma will become apparent not only in ourselves but also in our environment.

Establishing Buddhahood as our basic life tendency does not mean we rid ourselves of the other nine worlds. All these states are integral and necessary aspects of life. Without experiencing the sufferings of hell ourselves, we could never feel true compassion for others. Without the instinctive desires represented by hunger and animality, we would forget to eat, sleep, and reproduce ourselves, and soon become extinct. Even if we establish Buddhahood as our fundamental life tendency, we will still continue to experience the joys and sorrows of the nine worlds. However, they will not control us, and we will not define ourselves in terms of them. Based on the life tendency of Buddhahood, our nine worlds will be harmonized and function to benefit both ourselves and those around us.

OUR LIVES ARE INSEPARABLE FROM OUR ENVIRONMENT

People have a tendency to regard the environment as something separate from themselves, and from the viewpoint of that which we can observe, we are justified in drawing this distinction. However, from the viewpoint of ultimate reality as taught in Buddhism, the individual and the environment are one and inseparable. The principle of the oneness of life and its environment describes how life manifests itself in both a living subject and an objective environment.

"Life" indicates a subjective "self" that experiences the karmic effects of past actions. The environment is the objective realm where the karmic effects of life take shape. Environment here does not mean one overall context in which all beings live. Each living being has his or her own unique environment in which the effects of karma appear. The effects of one's karma, both good and bad, manifest themselves both in one's self and in the environment, because these are two integral phases of the same entity.

Since both life and its environment are one, whichever of the Ten Worlds an individual manifests internally will be mirrored in his or her environment. For example, a person in the state of hell will perceive the environment to be hellish, while a person in the world of animality will perceive the same environment as a jungle where only the strong survive.

This idea has important implications. First, as already mentioned, we need not seek enlightenment in a particular place. Wherever we are, under whatever circumstances, we can bring forth our innate Buddhahood through the Buddhist practice, thus transforming our experience of our environment into the Buddha's land. This is an act of freedom whereby we liberate ourselves from control by circumstances. For example, if we sufficiently elevate our condition of life, we will not be crushed by adversity but can command the strength and wisdom to use it constructively for our own development.

Moreover, as we accumulate good karma through Buddhist practice, the effects of this karma will become apparent not only in ourselves but also in our environment, in the form of improved material circumstances, greater respect from others, and so forth.

From this standpoint, one's environment stretches out to encompass the whole dimension of space. Our enlightenment is therefore not confined to ourselves but exerts an influence on our families, communities, nations, and ultimately all humanity. The principle of the oneness of life and its environment is the rationale for asserting that the Buddhist practice of individuals will work a transformation in society.

Society can be transformed by our Buddhist practice.

Buddhism expands the entire reality of life and shows the way to live a winning life—the most fulfilled existence.

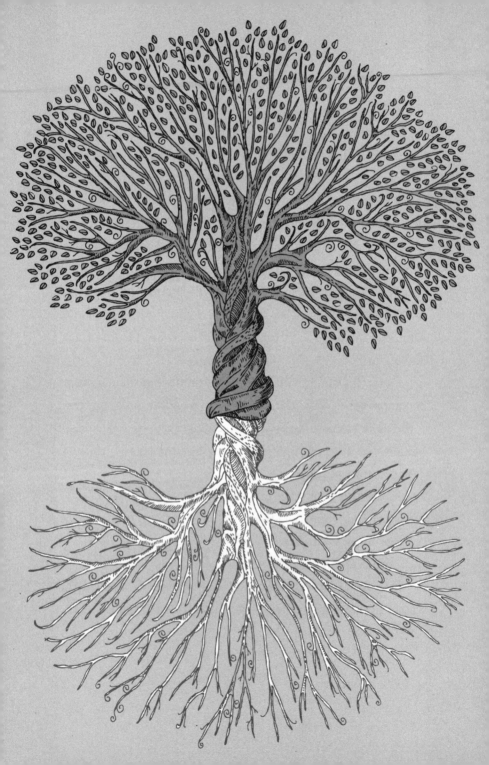

The Roots

BUDDHISM IS ONE OF THE WORLD'S OLDEST religions. At its core are the quests to understand life and to help people overcome their basic sufferings. Nichiren Buddhism traces its origins to the teachings of Shakyamuni, who is said to have lived some 2,500 years ago. Known as Siddhartha Gautama in his youth, at age nineteen he was a royal heir in India. His palace life was far removed from the everyday life of common people, and when

Nichiren Buddhism traces its origins to the teachings of Shakyamuni.

he discovered how people suffered outside the palace walls, he set out to discover how to overcome the roots of basic human suffering.

He made it his life's purpose to find solutions to the inescapable sufferings of life. He sought the foremost teachers of his day and practiced the extreme forms of asceticism they advocated as the means to realize the ultimate reality of life. After following their teachings for several years, and on the point of death

The wisdom of the Middle Way is neither the extreme of austerity nor of indulgence.

from fasting, Shakyamuni realized that their path was too extreme. He awakened to the wisdom of the Middle Way, neither the extreme of austerity nor of indulgence.

After accepting food from a young girl, he sat down under the bodhi (a pipal) tree. There he entered a profound meditation and finally attained enlightenment. He began at once to teach anyone who would listen. He would engage admirer and objector alike in dialogue and discourse to convey his awareness and insight into the human condition.

Since the depth of Shakyamuni's understanding far surpassed that of even the most learned of his day, he had to prepare his listeners by first teaching them more easily understood doctrines, using parables and everyday analogies in the process. In this way, he could elevate the life condition of those he taught, while always holding to his ultimate aim of showing people that they inherently possessed Buddhahood and could develop the qualities needed to conquer their sufferings.

The Buddha taught that everyone could conquer their sufferings.

For some forty years following his awakening at age thirty, Shakyamuni imparted to others portions of his own enlightenment. During the final eight years of his life, he expounded his ultimate teachings, which were later compiled as the Lotus Sutra.

THE LOTUS SUTRA

The Lotus Sutra is unique among the teachings of Buddhism because it affirms that enlightenment is possible for all people without distinction of race, gender, social standing, or education. Buddhism, as epitomized in the Lotus Sutra, is a powerful, life-affirming, egalitarian, and humanistic teaching.

Following Shakyamuni's passing, various schools of Buddhism spread throughout Asia. It was only natural that a broad range of interpretive schools should emerge, since in his fifty-year teaching career, he had employed a wide variety of means by which to transmit his enlightenment to people of various capacities and circumstances.

The Lotus Sutra gained particular prominence as it spread through Central Asia into China, the Korean Peninsula, and Japan. At the same time, however, confusion began to reign as to the true nature of Buddhism and the relative superiority of the sutras. To solve the problem, leading minds of the time compared and systematized the various teachings.

Lotus Sutra scroll, mid-seventeenth-century Japan

Eventually a scholar from China called Chih-i (later known as the Great Teacher T'ien-t'ai) developed a definitive standard by which to judge them. This standard classified Shakyamuni's teachings according to the order in which he expounded them, the nature of the particular doctrine taught in each sutra, and the method of its exposition. By classifying the teachings in this manner, T'ien-t'ai clarified that all the sutras were means of preparation for the highest teaching, the Lotus Sutra.

A BUDDHIST REFORMER

It was Nichiren Daishonin in Japan, however, who took the final all-important step to transform profound theory into a simple practice and thereby enable ordinary people to reveal their noblest state of life in the midst of day-to-day realities.

Nichiren realized his purpose was to reveal this ultimate truth to the people of his time and for all eternity. Hence, Nichiren Buddhism is for the present age, and

Nichiren Daishonin

Shakyamuni and T'ien-t'ai prepared the way.

Nichiren Daishonin lived from 1222 to 1282 during a tumultuous time of social unrest and natural catastrophe. The son of a fisherman, he became a religious acolyte and, after a period of intensive study, he came to realize that the Lotus Sutra constitutes the heart of Buddhist teachings.

He also brought it out of the realm of theoretical contemplation into an actual experiential practice when he first chanted Nam-myoho-renge-kyo (devotion to the Mystic Law) on April 28, 1253, and later inscribed the Gohonzon (the physical object of devotion).

He subsequently dedicated his life to sharing his realization, despite facing numerous persecutions for preaching what was considered a subversive doctrine. By declaring that embracing this Law had the power to allow all individuals to attain enlightenment, Nichiren disturbed the ruling class of politicians and priests who adhered to other forms of Buddhism. Nonetheless, he gained a loyal following of believers. He especially embraced ordinary people from all walks of life.

After Nichiren Daishonin's passing, his closest disciple, Nikko, kept the true spirit of Nichiren's teachings alive. For the next six centuries, Nichiren Buddhism was maintained by a relatively small religious group until the early part of the twentieth century.

A MODERN MOVEMENT

Tsunesaburo Makiguchi (1871–1944), an educator in Japan, was passionately dedicated to the reform of the Japanese educational system, which emphasized rote learning over critical independent thinking. He strove to develop modes of education that would unleash the potential of the individual. After studying Nichiren Daishonin's teachings, he realized that they could provide the philosophical underpinnings for the value-creating education that had been his lifetime goal.

Tsunesaburo Makiguchi

In 1928, Mr. Makiguchi committed himself to practicing this Buddhism along with a young teacher, Josei Toda (1900–58), whom he had met in 1920. In 1930, they founded the Soka Kyoiku Gakkai, or "Value-Creating Education Society," as a laypersons' organization, drawing its membership principally from among fellow educators.

Japan was then plunging headlong into war, a course diametrically opposed to the Buddhist reverence for life. As World War II progressed, the militarist government redoubled its efforts to crack down on all forms of dissidence. Mr. Makiguchi and Mr. Toda found themselves under increasing pressure to compromise their beliefs and practice the state religion of Shintoism.

Even the priests with whom Mr. Makiguchi and Mr. Toda associated faltered in their faith. The government asked these priests to accept a Shinto talisman and enshrine it at their head temple. This would be in direct contradiction with the teachings and spirit of Nichiren Daishonin. The priests, fearful of their own safety and wanting to curry favor with the authorities, accepted this governmental order so as to protect themselves from persecution.

Makiguchi resisted government persecution, refusing to compromise his beliefs.

Mr. Makiguchi, however, refused to violate the spirit of Nichiren Buddhism. His resistance to the government order led to his and Mr. Toda's arrest and imprisonment as "thought criminals" in 1943 along with other Soka Kyoiku Gakkai leaders.

Mr. Makiguchi, at seventy-two, endured brutality and

privation in prison, refusing on all counts to compromise his convictions. The records of his interrogations reveal a man propounding, without a trace of hesitation or fear, the very thoughts that had led to his incarceration. On November 18, 1944, he died at seventy-three in the Tokyo Detention House. (Visit www.tmakiguchi.org for more information.)

POSTWAR DEVELOPMENT

Josei Toda survived the ordeal and was released on July 3, 1945, just weeks before Japan's surrender. The Soka Kyoiku Gakkai had all but disintegrated under wartime persecution. Though physically ravaged by two years in prison, Mr. Toda immediately set about rebuilding the organization. It was renamed the Soka Gakkai (Value Creation Society).

Josei Toda

Mr. Toda resolved that the mission of this new organization should not be confined to the field of education but rather that it be expanded to the betterment of society as a whole. The Soka Gakkai rapidly grew under Josei Toda's leadership to more than 750,000 households by the time of his death in 1958. (Visit www.joseitoda.org for more information.)

DAISAKU IKEDA

Josei Toda's responsibilities were assumed by Daisaku Ikeda, who became the third president on May 3, 1960. Mr. Ikeda had met Mr. Toda at age nineteen and committed himself to practicing the ideals of the Soka Gakkai, making Mr. Toda his mentor.

Mr. Ikeda has dedicated himself continually to fulfilling the visions Mr. Toda shared with him in the areas of peace, culture, and education, based on Nichiren's teachings. Through his international travels beginning in 1960, Mr. Ikeda has contributed greatly to Buddhism becoming a truly global religion. In 1975, the Soka Gakkai International was formed, and today, Nichiren Buddhism is being practiced by more than 12 million people in 192 countries and territories under the auspices of the SGI.

Daisaku Ikeda

The American organization, called the SGI-USA, was formed in 1960 when Mr. Ikeda visited the United States. (Visit www.daisakuikeda.org for more information.)

AN ASSOCIATION FOR PEACE

The SGI believes that the development of peace, culture, and education is essential to building a better world. Centered on this ideal, the SGI carries out activities globally. In 1957, Josei Toda issued a declaration against the use of nuclear weapons, labeling them criminal under any circumstances; and he called upon the youth of the world to work to abolish these weapons of mass destruction.

SGI believes the development of peace, culture, and education is essential to building a better world.

Taking up this challenge, the SGI, under Mr. Ikeda's leadership, has been working tirelessly to create the conditions for a peaceful world.

The efforts to fulfill Mr. Toda's vision of peace have resulted in the SGI's wide-ranging activities, for instance, as a nongovernmental organization with official ties to the United Nations. The SGI has sponsored public information programs that aim through exhibitions, symposia, and other forums to promote awareness of the issues of war and peace and the feasibility of peaceful alternatives. Major international exhibitions on such themes as disarmament, human rights, and environmental protection have traveled throughout the world bringing public awareness of these critical issues.

What happens when a nuclear bomb explodes?

The SGI-sponsored exhibition "Everything You Treasure—For a World Free From Nuclear Weapons" was on display at California Polytechnic State University, San Luis Obispo, California, March 2015.

Personally, Mr. Ikeda has engaged in dialogues with international academics and intellectuals like British historian Arnold J. Toynbee and with policymakers and political leaders such as Zhou Enlai, Corazon Aquino, Mikhail Gorbachev, and Nelson Mandela, exchanging ideas on how to create world peace and better understandings among people, and many other topics. He has received numerous awards and recognition from universities and nations around the world for his efforts to promote peace.

Applying the spirit of Buddhism to modern times, he has also founded several institutions dedicated to peace and intercultural dialogue. The Toda Institute for Global Peace

Mitsu Kimura

Soka University of America, Aliso Viejo, California

and Policy Research in Honolulu conducts independent research and networks with peace researchers, activists, and policymakers to provide a global forum for the discussion and implementation of cooperatively designed policy strategies. And the Ikeda Center for Peace, Learning, and Dialogue in Boston provides a venue for pooling wisdom and fostering dialogue among the world's peace-oriented cultural, philosophical, and religious traditions, thus developing a network of global citizens in the pursuit of peace.

Education has been of central concern to the Soka Gakkai since its inception, and many ideas set forth by Mr. Makiguchi and Mr. Toda have been brought to fruition through the Soka school system. From preschool to postgraduate, the Soka system undertakes education designed to stimulate wisdom and engagement within society. On May 3, 2001, Soka University of America opened as a nonsectarian liberal arts college in Southern California. (Visit www.soka.edu for more information.)

Soka education is designed to stimulate wisdom and engagement within society.

DISCUSSIONS OPEN TO ALL

At the heart of this global movement are discussion meetings. These neighborhood gatherings where people share experiences, encourage one another, and study Buddhism are the backbone of the SGI. They are forums where anyone can speak freely, ask questions, or simply sit and watch. Meetings are held regularly in homes or in SGI-USA Buddhist centers. The activities are free and anyone is welcome to attend and participate.

Nichiren Buddhism is truly a religion that crosses all boundaries, with a diversity rarely seen in other institutions. This is proof that by overcoming our impasses, by winning over our own lack of understanding and constantly striving to awaken the Buddha nature inside us, we can build a lasting world peace.

There is no way to legislate, dictate, or force peace onto humanity. As Daisaku Ikeda writes in the foreword to his book *The Human Revolution*: "A great human revolution in just a single individual will help achieve a change in the destiny of a nation and, further, will enable a change in the destiny of all humankind."

In our jigsaw-puzzle world, then, it soon becomes obvious that through each person becoming truly happy and helping others to do the same, society will change.

By awakening the Buddha nature inside each of us, we can build a lasting world peace.

This is Buddhism's blueprint for peace, or what we call *kosen-rufu*, the compassionate movement to share widely the wonderful philosophy of Nichiren Buddhism. The only way for people to live together in peace is for many individuals to awaken to the need for an inner revolution. For one happy person's influence on his or her environment will have a profound and lasting effect.

Visit www.sgi-usa.org for more information and to find a discussion meeting near you.

Frequently Asked Questions

WHAT IS ENLIGHTENMENT?

THE WORD *ENLIGHTENMENT* CALLS TO MIND those who practice austerities and thereby gain extraordinary powers beyond the reach of common mortals. Nichiren Daishonin, however, taught that enlightenment, or Buddhahood, is a condition of life accessible to everyone, under any circumstances, by chanting Nam-myoho-renge-kyo.

It is only our inability to believe this—what we call our fundamental darkness or delusion—that prevents us from calling forth our Buddhahood.

Buddhahood is a condition of life accessible to everyone under any circumstances.

Nichiren explains: "When deluded, one is called an ordinary being, but when enlightened, one is called a Buddha. This is similar to a tarnished mirror that will shine like a jewel when polished. A mind now clouded by the illusions of the innate darkness of life is like a tarnished mirror, but when polished, it is sure to become like a clear mirror, reflecting the essential nature of phenomena and the true aspect of reality. Arouse deep faith, and diligently polish your mirror day and night. How should you polish it? Only by chanting Nam-myoho-renge-kyo" (*The Writings of Nichiren Daishonin*, vol. 1, p. 4).

We "arouse deep faith" by chanting Nam-myoho-renge-kyo to the Gohonzon with the firm conviction that we already possess Buddhahood.

We "arouse deep faith" by chanting Nam-myoho-renge-kyo to the Gohonzon with the firm conviction that we already possess Buddhahood. This conviction overrides our habits and preconceived attitudes, enabling us to call forth the Buddha's courage, compassion, and wisdom, which we can apply to any circumstance. Even the daily challenges we face head-on become the means by which we can live fulfilled, happy lives.

Using the analogy of a lion, Nichiren describes how this powerful animal unleashes the same force "whether he traps a tiny ant or attacks a fierce animal" (*The Writings of Nichiren*

Daishonin, vol. 1, p. 412). Our inherent Buddhahood is the source of limitless power and wisdom that enables us to tackle any situation, however big or small, and guides us toward the best course of action.

Enlightenment is not a fixed state we someday achieve. Rather, it is a lifelong process of challenge and renewal—a vigilant championing of the inherent dignity of life through thought, word, and action.

DOES NICHIREN BUDDHISM WORK FOR EVERYONE?

Nichiren Buddhism teaches that the potential for Buddhahood exists in all people without exception. All people also possess the potential for delusion, specifically the delusion that they are incapable of experiencing the indestructible happiness that comes with enlightenment. The practice of Buddhism is the means by which to discard delusion and reveal the Buddhahood within.

Awakening the Buddhahood in all people, not merely a select group, is the solemn vow of a Buddha. The Lotus Sutra articulates this vow in a passage we recite morning and evening as part of our Nichiren Buddhist practice, "At all times I think to myself: How can I cause living beings to gain entry into the unsurpassed way and quickly acquire the body of a Buddha?" (*The Lotus Sutra and Its Opening and Closing Sutras*, p. 273).

Awakening the Buddhahood in all people is the solemn vow of a Buddha.

Because Buddhism is based on profound universal compassion, adopting its principles will result in benefit for all, regardless of whether they are actually Buddhist practitioners. The greatest fortune, however, derives from real dedication to the three fundamentals, or pillars, of our teaching: faith, practice, and study.

IS IT OK TO PRACTICE EVEN THOUGH I DON'T KNOW THAT I BELIEVE IN IT?

Many people are wary of how some religions tend to emphasize belief without any evidence of how they work. They basically ask for your blind faith. Nichiren Buddhism is different. It is a philosophy and practice of actual proof—belief, or faith, arises from the positive impact the practice has on people's lives, from how it leads to happiness here and now.

Belief, or faith, arises from the positive impact the practice has on people's lives, from how it leads to happiness here and now.

Of course, if you are very new to chanting Nam-myoho-renge-kyo, you might not have experienced any conspicuous actual proof yet. But at SGI-USA activities, you have no doubt heard members' experiences of having received benefit as well as explanations of how the practice works. This can be your starting point—instead of blind faith, you can begin with an *expectation* that the practice works and therefore be willing to try it.

As Nichiren Buddhists, we develop ever-deepening faith through our own experience rather than simply accepting our beliefs from others. Ours is a philosophy of proof, and new members can expect to see actual proof from their practice soon after starting.

WHY DO WE HAVE TO CHANT? WHY NOT JUST MEDITATE OR THINK POSITIVELY?

Chanting Nam-myoho-renge-kyo reveals our Buddha nature. It directly connects our lives to the fundamental rhythm of the universe that we refer to as the Mystic Law.

Nichiren Daishonin teaches: "If you wish to free yourself from the sufferings of birth and death you have endured since time without beginning and to attain without fail unsurpassed enlightenment in this lifetime, you must perceive the mystic truth that is originally inherent in all living beings. This truth is Myoho-renge-kyo. Chanting Myoho-renge-kyo will therefore enable you to grasp the mystic truth innate in all life" (*The Writings of Nichiren Daishonin,* vol. 1, p. 3).

"Chanting Myoho-renge-kyo will therefore enable you to grasp the mystic truth innate in all life."

This passage expresses the main difference between chanting and the internalized disciplines of meditation or positive thinking. Although meditation and positive thinking are helpful for many people, these practices are centered on the mind—calming it and training it—and cannot express the fundamental nature of our lives, the enlightened, highest condition of our lives as a whole. Nichiren Buddhism teaches that the Buddhahood inside us far transcends the power of our minds. It is the power of life itself that we tap into to transform our entire lives.

Our thinking does become more positive as a result of chanting, but this is because chanting Nam-myoho-renge-kyo draws out Buddhahood from the depths of our lives, which naturally changes our ways of thinking. The emergence of Buddhahood becomes the positive basis of every aspect of our lives, both mental and physical.

IF I CHANT, WILL MY
PROBLEMS GO AWAY?

A consistent theme of earlier Buddhist teachings was that problems and the desires that underlie them must be completely eradicated in order for one to experience absolute happiness, or Buddhahood.

Nichiren Buddhism is not about making problems go away—it is about transforming them into sources of value creation and benefit. This is explained by the key concept that "earthly desires are enlightenment." The term *earthly desires* includes all the workings of life that cause one psychological and physical suffering; in other words, both the things we wish to rid ourselves of and the things

Nichiren Buddhism does not make problems go away—it transforms them into sources of value creation and benefit.

we long for. As practitioners of Nichiren Buddhism, we acknowledge and accept—even celebrate—the fact that we are ordinary people filled with a wide variety of desires.

As Nichiren Daishonin explains, "[When Nichiren and his followers recite Nam-myoho-renge-kyo], they are burning the firewood of earthly desires, summoning up the wisdom fire of bodhi or enlightenment" (*The Record of the Orally Transmitted Teachings*, p. 11). We chant about our problems not only to resolve them but to create within ourselves an indestructible joy and appreciation of life.

Without having any problems to face, we would simply run out of gas, with little motivation to challenge our lives and reveal our Buddhahood.

DO NICHIREN BUDDHISTS BELIEVE IN GOD?

The answer to whether Nichiren Buddhists believe in God can be yes . . . or no. It all depends on one's definition of "God." Certainly, there is a kinship between the one God (as defined by the beliefs of Judaism, Christianity, and Islam) and Buddhism's concept of the "Mystic Law."

The Mystic Law, Nam-myoho-renge-kyo, gives rise to all phenomena in the universe, from the galaxies and planets, to the water, trees, and each of us. The same power that creates the stars lies within us, with every

> *The Mystic Law, Nam-myoho-renge-kyo, gives rise to all phenomena in the universe.*

human being equally having the potential to lead a life of ultimate fulfillment—to overcome all obstacles and change all hardships into joys.

The Mystic Law is both "out there" and inside our own lives; it permeates everything and everyone. Buddhas are human beings who perceive the Mystic Law within and fully manifest it in their daily lives. In this sense, there is no absolute distinction between the Mystic Law and us human beings. We are all Buddhas worthy of supreme respect.

We can use the limitless power of the Mystic Law to work for our benefit, but it is not something we beseech to answer our prayers.

While we acknowledge the existence of this power of life itself, at the same time we remain firmly at the controls. The degree to which we can tap the power of the Law depends on the strength of our faith and practice.

When we chant Nam-myoho-renge-kyo with confidence, we activate the Mystic Law within us. Thus, armed with a strong life condition, we become the catalyst for everything in our lives—people, things, situations—to function in support of achieving our desires and our deepest happiness.

Rather than encouraging dependence on either an external power or on an individual's inherent ability, Nichiren Buddhism perfectly balances the two. This fusion of the macrocosm (the universal Law) and the microcosm (the individual) gives rise to an individual's happiness, much like the fusion of wick and wax allows a candle to burn and shed light.

Much of the above explanation of the Mystic Law may sound familiar to those who believe in the God of the Bible. And indeed, when first beginning to practice Nichiren Buddhism, many say that Nichiren Daishonin's teachings are what they've always believed.

Ultimately, of course, ours is not a monotheistic religion. We don't believe in a creator god, distinct from us. We do embrace the view of a compassionate life of the universe. We identify the highest potential in all human life and continually strive to reveal this potential both in ourselves and in those around us.